Caryl S. Parrott

A descriptive reading on Egypt

Vol. VII

Caryl S. Parrott

A descriptive reading on Egypt
Vol. VII

ISBN/EAN: 9783337240233

Printed in Europe, USA, Canada, Australia, Japan

Cover: Foto ©ninafisch / pixelio.de

More available books at **www.hansebooks.com**

A

DESCRIPTIVE READING

ON

EGYPT

ILLUSTRATED BY FIFTY LANTERN
SLIDES

WILLIAM H. RAU
PHILADELPHIA
1890

ILLUSTRATIONS.

1. Port Said and the Entrance to the Suez Canal.
2. The Suez Canal.
3. Harbor of Alexandria.
4. Pompey's Pillar, Alexandria.
5. Mahmoudieh Canal.
6. A Street in Cairo.
7. Shoubra Palace.
8. Interior of an Arabic Palace, Cairo.
9. Masharabeah—Lattice Window.
10. Fountain of Ablution—Mosque of Hassan.
11. Bazaar of Antiques, Cairo.
12. Interior of Gezeereh Palace, Cairo.
13. Citadel and Mosque of Mohamed Ali.
14. Arab Cemetery in the Desert.
15. Tombs of the Caliphs, Cairo.
16. Water Carriers.
17. Ra-em-ke—Oldest Wooden Statue.)
18. Mummy of Rameses II.
19. The Mahmal Leaving for Mecca.
20. Group of Great Pyramids.
21. Temple Sphynx and Great Pyramid.
22. The Sphynx Excavated.
23. Pyramid of Sakkarah.
24. Siout from the Nile.
25. Colonnade, Temple of Denderah.
26. Trading Boat on the Nile.
27. The Grand Temple, Luxor.
28. General View of Luxor.
29. A Mummy Dealer.
30. Avenue of Sphynxes and Propylon, Karnak.
31. The Great Hall of Columns, Karnak.
32. General View of the Great Temple, Karnak.
33. The Colossi—Thebes.

34. Great Court, Medinet Aboo.
35. The Rameseum Grand Hall, Thebes.
36. Valley of the Tombs of the Kings.
37. Pylons of the Temple, Edfoo.
38. The Harbor of Assouan.
39. First Cataract of the Nile.
40. Philæ from the Cataract.
41. The Ruins of Philæ.
42. Ruins of the Mosque Mischod.
43. Shadoof and Sakkieh.
44. Gertasse.
45. Nubian Boy Riding Buffalo.
46. Kirscheh.
47. Temple and Desert, Wady Saboah.
48. Great Temple, Aboo Simbel.
49. Interior of Great Temple.
50. Second Cataract of the Nile.

EGYPT.

EGYPT! What memories sweep o'er us at the mention of that name! Before the mature mind grasps the magnitude of the wonders it recalls, the child-mind passes back to the days when its first interest centered in the infant Moses, saved from the wrath of the wicked Pharaoh; in Joseph, made second in power in the kingdom; the death of the first-born and the bondage and escape of the people of Israel. And thus, before the interest of the student-mind is enlisted, that of the child is caught by the wonder of its story. And can we doubt that a land that has laid its charm upon us when children will lose its hold on us now? A land whose age is not counted by years or even hundreds of years, but by thousands,—until we are lost in antiquity; the first cradle of the human race, the oldest theatre in which the great drama of life was played. Here the arts and sciences had birth, and literature and religion sprang into existence. Her schools of learning flourished before Greece had breathed, or Rome been even dreamed of, and her architectural achievements are to-day the wonder of the civilized world.

1. Port Said and the Entrance to the Suez Canal.—From the mouth of the Damietta branch of the Nile to the Gulf of Pelusium there stretches a low belt of sand, varying in width from two hundred to three hundred yards, and serving to separate the Mediterranean from the waters of Lake Menzaleh, though often, when the lake is full and the waves of the Mediterranean are high, the two meet across this slight boundary line. In the beginning of the month of April, 1859, a small body of men, the pioneers of the Suez Canal landed at that spot of this narrow sandy slip, which had been chosen as the starting point of the canal from the Mediterranean, and the site of the city and port intended ultimately to rival Alexandria. It owed its selection not to its being the spot from which the shortest line across the Isthmus could be drawn, but to its being that point of the coast to which deep water approached the nearest. This spot was called Port Said, in honor of the Viceroy.

The first thing to be done was to make the ground on which to build the future town. This was done by dredging in the shallows of the lake, close to the belt of sand ; the same operation serving at once to form an inner port, and to extend the area and raise the height of the dry land. When the native laborers were withdrawn and recourse had to machinery, great impetus was given to Port Said. It soon became, perhaps, the largest workshop in the world.

Thus sprang up in a few years, on a site most disadvantageous, a town of nearly ten thousand inhabitants, regularly laid out in streets and squares, with docks, quays, churches, hospitals, mosques, hotels, and all the adjuncts of a sea-port, and with the most easily-approached and safest harbor along the coast.

2. The Suez Canal.—Notwithstanding the attempts before made, it was reserved to our century, with its enormous technical resources, to solve the problem of joining the Mediterranean to the Red Sea in a way which wholly excludes any further fear of its being closed by neglect or the action of the elements. A Frenchman of genius and determination, Monsieur de Lesseps, during the tedium of a quarantine, read an essay by La Pere, which led to his forming the resolution so pregnant with results to the whole commercial world, to attempt to cut through the Isthmus of Suez.

On the 25th of April, 1859, Monsieur de Lesseps, surrounded by ten or fifteen Europeans, and some one hundred native workmen, gave the first stroke of the spade to the future highway between the Mediterranean and the Red Sea. Hard indeed must have been the life of the first workers on this desolate slip of land, and the powers of endurance of the little band were often sorely tried. All the world knows how the plan succeeded, but the enormous difficulties which had to be overcome are not so well known, nor how the Pacha from the first supported the scheme, and how intelligently and devotedly he was seconded by the Khedive. In 1868, in spite of the opposition of English statesmen, and the distrust of the whole European world of finance, the canal was so far completed that steamships of moderate size could pass through it, and the Viceroy Ismail held a festival of inauguration, which exceeded in splendor everything in the way of hospitality and entertainment that had been seen within the past century. Besides princes and grandees he bade the

representatives of the press from all parts of the
globe as his guests, and in the course of a few days,
as if by magic, the attention of every man, near and
far, great and small, was centered on the Suez Canal.

At the present day a constantly-increasing number
of ships of every nation incessantly navigate it, and
the maintenance of this great monument of enterprise and skill is absolutely secure.

3. Harbor of Alexandria.—From whichever side
it is approached the coast of Egypt is exceedingly
low. There is nothing at all remarkable in the view
of Alexandria from the sea ; the town looks like a
long horizontal streak of whitewash, mingled with
brown, and crossed perpendicularly with the sharp
line of ships' masts, but she occupies a strong position
and posesses great commercial advantages. No sit-
uation could be more commanding, few harbors are
more secure and capacious, and thousands of ships
ride upon her blue waters. As you enter the harbor on
the right are the island and tower of Pharos ; on the
left are rocks and the promontory of Lochias, where
the palace stands ; one of the most prominent
objects is the new lighthouse on the point of Eunos-
tus, in which is a revolving light, visible at a distance
of twenty miles.

As soon as the steamer anchors in the harbor it is
surrounded by numbers of boats, rowed by men of all
colors save white, and dressed some in the Greek and
some in the Turkish ostume, calling out in gutteral
Arabic and broken English and Italian for passen-
gers. It is in these boats that the traveler obtains
his first experience of the ways of the natives ; mid-
way between the vessel and the shore they will stop

rowing, make an exorbitant charge, and demand immediate payment. Talk is useless, but a peremptory order and a threatened blow will cause them to sink down in submission and row steadily to shore, where they will gratefully accept about one-third the amount they attempted to extort.

4. **Pompey's Pillar, Alexandria.**—There is little in the present city to remind us of the ancient glory of Alexandria—so illustrous as the seat of learning. To-day a city of extremes and contrasts. Deluged in winter by rain, and at times even pinched by cold, it is annually scorched for five months by a fierce sun, dusted by desert sand, and parched by drought. A cosmopolitan city of French houses, Italian villas, Turkish latticed-windowed buildings, and native mud hovels; a city where every tongue is commonly spoken, and every coin is in current circulation.

The most striking monumental relic of Alexandria is the column erroneously called "Pompey's Pillar." It stands upon an eminence which was probably the highest ground of the ancient city, and commands an interesting view of Lake Mareotis and the modern city. The column is nearly one hundred feet in height, the shaft (of a single granite block) being seventy-three feet, and the lofty pedestal occupying the rest of the height. The substructions were once under the level of the ground, and formed part of a paved area; the stones of which have been removed, leaving only those beneath the column itself, to the great risk of the monument.

Much controversy has been occasioned by the name given this pillar; some have supposed that this was one of the four hundred columns that belonged to the great library; others have derived it from *Pompaios*, as having served for a landmark, and others endeavored to read in the inscription the name of Pompey. It is now proven that it was erected by Publius, the Prefect of Egypt, in honor of the Roman emperor, Diocletian.

5. Mahmoudieh Canal.—Traveling from Alexandria to Cairo, most of the journey is made in a small steamboat on the far-famed Mahmoudieh Canal. The right bank of the canal is bordered for some distance with the houses and gardens of the wealthy inhabitants of Alexandria, and is the fashionable afternoon promenade. Many of the gardens are well worth seeing for the beauty and luxuriance of the shrubs and flowers.

As the canal runs through the Delta it is elevated by banks above the surrounding country, and one can see in every direction Arab villages, like so many square or circular mud heaps, rising upon every mound, and secured by walls of earth against the annual incursions of the Nile.

The canal is about seventy miles in length, and, connecting Alexandria with a branch of the Nile, makes the water communication with Cairo perfect. In the greatness and cruelty of its accomplishment this canal may vie with the gigantic labors of the Pharaohs. Two hundred and fifty thousand people, men, women and children, were swept from the villages of the Delta and heaped like a ridge along the destined banks of that fatal canal. They had provisions for only one month, and implements they had few or none; but the Pasha's command was urgent,— the men worked with all the energy of despair, and stabbed into the ground as if it were their enemy; children carried away the soil in little handfuls, mothers laid their infants on the shelterless banks, the scourge kept all to work. Famine soon made its appearance, and it was a fearful sight to see that great multitude convulsively working against time; as a dying horse bites the ground in its agony, they tore up that great grave. Twenty-five thousand people perished, but the given contract was completed, and in six weeks the waters of the Nile were led to Alexandria.

6. A Street in Cairo.—It is to be doubted whether Bagdad itself is more truly Oriental than Cairo; here it is that the traveler begins to feel that he is really in the East. The houses are high and narrow, with upper stories projecting; from these jut windows of delicate lattice-work of old brown wood, like big bird cages. Many of the streets are very narrow, and are roofed in overhead with long rafters and pieces of matting, through which stray dusty sunbeams.

In the principal thoroughfares the crowd ebbs and flows unceasingly—a noisy, changing, restless tide—half Oriental, half European; on foot, on horseback, and in carriages. Here are Syrian dragomans in baggy trousers and braided jackets, barefooted Egyptian fellaheen, in ragged blue shirts and felt skull-caps; Greeks in stiff white tunics; Persians with high caps of dark woven stuffs; swarthy Bedouins in flowing garments; Englishmen in palm-leaf hats and knickerbockers, dangling their long legs across almost invisible donkeys; Armenian priests in long black gowns and high, square caps; native women of the poorer class in black veils that leave only the eyes uncovered, and long, trailing garments; majestic ghosts of Algerian Arabs, all in white. Now comes a sweetmeat vendor, with his tray; now an Egyptian lady on a large gray donkey, led by a servant, with a showy sabre at his side. The lady wears a rose-colored silk dress and white veil, beside the black silk outer garment, which being cloak, hood and veil all in one, fills out with the wind as she rides, like a balloon. She sits astride, her feet in their violet velvet slippers just resting on the stirrups. Nor is the steed less well dressed than the mistress; his high-pommeled saddle is resplendent with velvet and embroidery; and his headgear is all tags, tassels and fringes.

7. Shoubra Palace.—The Shoubra Palace, one of the country residences built for Mohammed Ali, lies about four miles out of Cairo. The road to it is broad and level, bordered on both sides by trees which meet overhead, and form a complete arbor for the whole distance. Here little sheds of roadside cafes alternate with smart modern villas; gardeners' lads with a bouquet stuck in their turbans, offer flowers for sale to the passer-by. Ragged fellaheen on jaded donkeys trot side by side with elegant attachés on high-stepping Arab steeds; while tourists in hired carriages, Jew bankers in smart phaetons, veiled ladies of the harem in London-built broughams, Italian shopkeepers in fashionable toilets, officers in braided frocks, and English girls in tall hats and close-fitting habits, pass and repass, preceed and follow each other in one changing, restless stream, the like of which is to be seen in no other capital in the world. The gardens of the palace are extensive, and are laid out in squares, and planted with orange and lemon trees. The extensive summer-house is built in the form of a hollow square, the interior of which is a reservoir with a fountain in the centre. The arcades and kiosks surrounding the basin have a very fine appearance. The broad marble walk opens upon the gardens except at the four corners, where there are billiard and smoking rooms.

8. Interior of an Arabic Palace, Cairo.—There are no old palaces at Cairo ; all are of modern date and of the Saracenic style of architecture ; but into their construction has been put all the charm of beauty and romance that Oriental luxury could devise. The slender, airy columns, whose graceful proportions are borrowed from the native palm tree, and the beautiful serrated arches are of purest alabaster. The square court is filled with tropical plants, and in the centre is the fountain, whose faint plashing makes pleasant music. The floor of the corridor is of inlaid marble, while the walls are of rich tiling. Beyond we see the delicate tracery of the lattice-window, which opens into the richly furnished reception-room. The floor is covered with heavy turkish carpet, and luxurious divans extend around the room. While resting there we may study the details of the richly decorated ceiling, the beautiful patterns of the earthenware tiles which line the lower part of the walls, and the elegantly carved brackets and shelves, on which are arranged all kinds of finely wrought vessels.

9. Masharabeah—Lattice Window.—" To wander through Cairo is to meet constant novelty ; only to look round is a joy, and merely to see is to learn." Not a little of the magical charm of this marvellous city is due to the Masharabeah. Leaving the carefully watered footway of a street on both sides of which are ranged handsome houses of European architecture, we turn into a shady side street, where we walk between two high stone walls. Not a window allows of any friendly intercourse between the street and the interior, but balconies with close lattices of wood-work project before us, behind us, above us; on the right hand and on the left, all along the street, concealing everything that lives and stirs within from the gaze of the passer-by or of the opposite neighbor. Through the interstices and openings of these lattices,—which are worked with richly pierced patterns and delicately turned bars,—many an Arab lady's eye peeps down on us below, for the lattice admits air to the women's rooms and allows the fair ones to see without being seen.

Behind this window is the harem, where even the most intimate friends of the master are forbidden to enter. The inhabitants devote their entire existence to the care of their children, to dress, to smoking their nargilehs, and to trifling amusements. They do not regard themselves in any sense as prisoners, and have frequently assured European ladies that ·they would not exchange places with them.

10. Fountain of Ablution—Mosque of Hassan. —The Mosque of Sultan Hassan, confessedly the most beautiful in Cairo, is also perhaps the most beautiful in the Moslem world. It was built at just that happy moment when Arabian art in Egypt having ceased merely to imitate, at length evolved an original style of its own. It may justly be regarded as the highest point reached by Saracenic art in Egypt.

Going up the steps and through a lofty hall, up more steps and along a gloomy corridor, we reach the great court. The first sight of this court is a surprise, and its beauty equals its novelty. An immense marble quadrangle, open to the sky and enclosed within lofty walls, with a vast recess at each side, framed in by a single arch. Each recess forms a spacious hall for rest and prayer ; that at the eastern end is wider and considerably deeper than the other three, and contains the holy niche and the pulpit of the preacher. There is a beautiful fountain in the court, at which each worshipper performs his ablutions on coming in. This done he leaves his slippers on the matting and treads the carpeted dais barefoot.

The dome shaped roof of the fountain is as light and fragile looking as a big bubble ; but what was once a miracle of Saracenic ornament is fast going to destruction. The rich marbles at its base are cracked and discolored, its stuccoed cupola is flaking off, its enamels are dropping out, and its lace-like wood tracery is shredding away by inches.

11. Bazaar of Antiques, Cairo.—To thoroughly enjoy an overwhelming impression of Orientel out-of-doors life, one should begin with a day in the native bazaars. The narrow thoroughfare is lined with little wooden shop-fronts, like open cabinets full of shelves, where the merchants sit in the midst of their goods, looking out at the passers-by and smoking in silence. Their apparel is most picturesque ; they wear ample white turbans, long vests of striped Syrian silk, and an outer robe of braided cloth or cashmere. That these stately beings should vulgarly buy and sell, seems altogether contrary to the eternal fitness of things. Their civility and patience are inexhaustible. One may turn over their whole stock and go away again and again without buying, and yet be always welcomed and dismissed with smiles. Many of the bazaars are very small, seeming like a cupboard fitted up with tiers of little drawers and pigeonholes. Our merchant in the picture has a much more commodious apartment, and makes a fine display of his goods on the pavement. Here may be bought beautiful cabinets of ebony inlaid with mother-of-pearl ; quaint little stools ; old embroideries ; beautiful specimens of the delicately wrought wood-work used in the lattice windows ; old porcelain ; and brass and copper vessels, cups, basins, trays, and incense burners, many of which are exquisitely engraved with Arabesque patterns or sentences from the poets. Strong-minded must be the foreigner who can pass this tempting display without stopping to purchase.

12. Interior of Gezeereh Palace, Cairo.—None of the palaces of the Khedive is more worthy of mention than the palace of Gezeereh—" the island" —being situated on an island in the Nile. It is a princely residence furnished with Oriental magnificence ; at the opening of the Suez Canal the Viceroy's most distinguished guests lived in it, and splendid balls attracted vast number. It contains chimney pieces of onyx which cost a fortune, and nothing prettier can be imagined than the room furnished with

light blue satin which was prepared for the Empress
Eugenie. Magnificent as is everything in this palace,
all else is forgotten when we see the Kiosk of
Gezeereh, for in splendor, charm and peculiarity it
leaves far behind it everything that has been produced
by Oriental architecture in modern times. The path
leading to this fairy palace is beautiful; and passing
a pool of translucent water, we see before us the
lightest and airiest of structures, a hall in the style of
the Alhambra. Lingering here in the cool evening
hour, soothed by the plashing of the fountains, inhal-
ing the fragrance of the flowers, one might dream on
forever.

13. Citadel and Mosque of Mohamed Ali.—This
citadel is in itself a small town, being a combination
of mosque, fortress, and palace, built upon a rocky
elevation commanding the city. The greatest and
most celebrated monument erected in Cairo by
Mohamed Ali is the mosque in which he lies entombed.
Its two tall and slender minarets are conspicuous
from a great distance, and as one leaves Cairo they
remain longer in sight than any other landmark. No
expense was spared in building this magnificent
structure; the beautiful alabaster which the ancient
Egyptians wrought in so many ways, was here so
lavishly employed that the building was called the
"Alabaster Mosque." The pale marble polish of this
stone gleams everywhere—in the court enclosed by
vaulted arcades, in the fountain rising in its midst,
and in the finely proportioned body of the mosque.

The view from the citadel is magnificent, the vast-
ness of the city, as it lies stretched below, surprises
everyone. It looks a perfect wilderness of flat roofs,

cupolas, minarets, and palm tops, with here and there an open space presenting the complete front of a mosque, gay groups of people and moving camels. You can plainly see as far southward as the Pyramids of Sakkarah, and trace the windings of the Nile for many miles across the plain.

Before leaving the visitor is shown the spot where the Mameluke nobles, four hundred and eighty in number, were shot down like dogs in a trap. One only is said to have escaped ; he leaped his horse over the wall, miraculously escaped unhurt, and fled to the desert.

14. Arab Cemetery in the Desert.— Leaving Cairo by the Gate of Victory we come at once to the hills that protect the city from the inroads of the desert. All is naked and barren, not a tree nor a particle of green to be seen. After riding for a mile or two over sandhills we reach one of the modern burial grounds of Cairo. There are a number of these cemeteries in and about the city, but this is by far the most extensive. In no instance is the graveyard enclosed, but frequently a small portion is walled in, with a building attached as a family tomb for some of the wealthier people.

Hardly has the Moslem breathed his last than the women set up their discordant wailing which sounds afar, and announces the melancholy event to the whole neighborhood. They beat their breasts, tear their hair, and continue their hideous cries, while the men of the household make the necessary preparations for the funeral on the morrow. When the time for the funeral arrives the procession moves through the streets at a good round pace until the mosque is

reached where a funeral prayer must be said. Then
the clamorous train hurries out to the cemetery in the
desert. The grave is already made,—a low structure
of bricks, with an arched top, open at one end. After
a short prayer, the body is taken from the bier, and
pushed into the opening so that it rests on the right
side, with the head towards Mecca. As soon as the
grave is closed bread, dates, and grease are distributed
among the poor who have in the meantime collected.
Then the procession disperses and the mourners return
to their homes. The grave of the departed remains
a bourne of pilgrimage, and his memory is perpet-
uated by the beautiful custom of distributing food to
the poor.

15. Tombs of the Caliphs, Cairo.—It is but a
short distance from this cemetery in the desert to the
tombs of the Mameluke Sultans, which are among
the most celebrated ruins of Cairo. They are usually
called by the inhabitants of the city El Kaidbai, the
name of the principal building, which is the tomb of
the nineteenth king of the dynasty, who was buried
here in 1496. There are a number of the tombs, each
of which consists of a building with a mosque attached.
The domes and minarets of many of them are exceedingly beautiful in design; the minarets being lofty
and graceful, and the domes covered with a raised fret-
work of arabesque patterns. The buildings are all of
light colored stone, laid in courses with black or red;
the black limestone is brought from the vicinity of the
convent of St. Anthony in the eastern desert; but the
red bands are merely painted on the originally light
surface.

No one can see these beautiful structures without regretting that they are permitted to go to decay; they are not merely neglected, but in many cases the materials have been taken for the erection of modern buildings. The mosques are shut, and the edifices connected with them are occupied by a few poor, ragged people.

16. Water Carriers.—Among the occupations that most forcibly strike the attention of the stranger in Cairo is that of the water carrier. On the road from Boulak to Cairo, the most peculiar feature of the scene is the immense number of these carriers constantly passing between the city and the port. Now we meet one bending under the load which is strapped across his shoulders, another may have the load on the back of a camel or donkey, and the next we meet may be a woman, walking with stately tread, as though the burden poised upon her head were a crown of gold.

The water is carried in skins, the legs being tied up, and the neck fitted with a brass cock ; occasionally the hair is left on, in which case, when nearly replenished, the skin has a horribly bloated and life-like appearance.

The water is sold from house to house, or peddled on the streets, the peddler attracting the attention of the passer-by by clattering the metal drinking cup and calling out, "The way of God, O thirsty ones."

Pious phrases, such as "God forgive thy sins, O distributor of drink !" or "God have mercy on thy parents !" are particularly frequent on the lips of the water seller when, in honor of some festival, he is hired to give water free of charge to all that ask it, and each one who receives the bowl of refreshing fluid at his hand responds with thanks, and a fervent "Amen" to his pious invocation. When the skin is empty the blessing of God is called down on the dispenser of drink, with the wish that he may come to Paradise.

17. Ra-em-ke. Oldest Wooden Statue.—Of all the known collections of Egyptian antiquities, that at Boulak is the most important, and can boast of one great advantage,—that for every object in it the place where it was found can be pointed out. Chief among these objects of interest is a very remarkable figure in sycamore wood. It is the oldest wooden statue in existence, and represents a high official of mature age. Ra-em-ke was a "superintendent of works," which probably means that he was an overseer of corvee labor at the building of the Great Pyramids. We seem to see him, staff in hand, watching his workmen. He belonged to the middle class, and his whole person expresses vulgar contentment and self-satisfaction; the body is stout and heavy, and the neck thick. The head, despite its vulgarity, does not lack energy. The eyes have a peculiarly life-like expression, the orbit having been cut out from the wood and the hollow filled with an eye composed of white and black enamel. The feet of the statue had perished, but have been restored.

By a curious coincidence the statue, which was found at Sakkarah, bore a striking resemblance to the local Sheykh-el-Beled or chief magistrate of the village. Always quick to seize upon the amusing side of an incident, the Arab diggers at once called the figure the "Sheykh-el-Beled," and it has retained the name ever since.

18. Mummy of Rameses II.—The central figure of Egyptian history has always been and always will be Rameses the Great. He it is, more than all the other Pharaohs, that excites our personal, living interest. He was the son of Seti I., the second Pharaoh of the nineteenth dynasty, and of the princess Tuaa, who is described on the monuments as "royal wife, róyal mother, and heiress and sharer of the throne." It is supposed that she had a better right than her husband to the double crown of Egypt, and that through her Rameses was born a king, equal in rank with his father; certain it is that he was accorded royal and divine honors from the hour of his birth. At the age of twelve he was formally associated with his father on the throne, and gradually assumed the cares of active government. Upon the death of his father he assumed the entire responsibility of the government, and immediately became famous for his battles. He conducted campaigns in Syria; he brought warfare into Ethiopia; he carried fire and sword into the land of Canaan and took, among other places, the strong fortresses of Ascalon and Jerusalem.

In the evening of his life it became his passion to build. He founded new cities, dug canals, built fortresses, multiplied statues, and erected most gorgeous and costly temples. No enterprise was too difficult, no project too vast for his ambition, and the remains of his efforts are the wonders of the world.

To-day all that is left of this precocious youth; this mighty warrior, terrible in battle; this supreme builder; this divine king;—occupies a small space in the Boulak Museum, numbered and labeled as an antique.

19. The Mahmal Leaving for Mecca.--The grandest festival of the Moslems is the departure of the Mahmal for Mecca. On that day all Cairo is astir the first thing in the morning. The streets leading from the citadel to the Bab-en-Nasr swarm with humanity; the shops are shut, and in every spot where the caravan will pass, heads piled behind heads crowd every window; Arabs and Nubians of every shade and description squeeze themselves in and out among the carriages, swarm to the top of every wall, and fill the air with laughter and pleasant greeting. Women in great numbers mix with the inquisitive throng, and dark eyes sparkle from every lattice window. On this occasion the curiosity and natural love of display innate in every Cairene is heightened by religious feeling, for the Mahmal is held in special veneration. Although it is a symbol of regal dignity only and has no religious significance, it has so often made the pilgrimage to Mecca, that it has assumed the character of a relic, of which the touch or even the sight brings a blessing.

The procession opens with a body of soldiers, proudly perched on tall camels; then a whole herd of the hump-backed beasts follow, decked with bells and stained orange color, bearing all the necessary baggage of the pilgrims; then follows some two hundred pilgrims on foot, chanting passages from the Koran; then a regiment of Egyptian infantry, followed by more pilgrims and a body of dervishes, carrying green banners embroidered with Arabic sentences in white and yellow. More bands, more infantry and more pilgrims follow. The people shout louder and louder; and now appears the great priest of the pilgrimage, who is entrusted with the leadership of the expedition. Behind him follow another troop of officers, dervishes and citizens; it seems as though the long stream would never end. Then occurs a break in the procession—an eager pause—a gathering murmur—and then, riding a gaunt dromedary at a rapid trot, his fat sides shaking and his head rolling at every step, appeared the famous "Sheykh of the Camel," the idol of the people, who makes the pilgrimage every year, and is supposed to fast and roll his head all the way to and from Mecca. Presently from afar a swelling roar makes itself heard; the noise increases; every eye is turned down the street in greatest excitement;—and presently we distinguish the sacred Mahmal. Everyone strives to touch it and benefit by its blessing. Handkerchiefs are let down from windows, that they may be sanctified by the sacred contact. The people scream and shout, and are fairly beside themselves with excitement, and all in honor of an empty litter, of gilded tracery, hung round with cloth richly embroidered with texts from the Koran. In the days of the Mamelukes the Mahmal represented the litter of the sultan, but now it simply carries the tribute-carpet, sent every year from Cairo to the tomb of the Prophet.

20. Group of Great Pyramids.—One of the first excursions while in Cairo will be a visit to the Pyramids. The fine road is well shaded by trees, and the dewy verdure of the fields very refreshing. All the time the pyramids are in sight, and it is singular to note the deception created by their great size and the clearness of the atmosphere. At first they appear neither very high nor very distant. From afar

the well-known triangular forms look small and
shadowy and are too familiar to be in any way startling; but when the edge of the desert is at last
reached and the platform gained, the effect is as
sudden as it is overwhelming. It is only when we
look at the immense pile above us, and observe that
the first course of the innumerable layers of huge
stones are nearly as high as a man, that we can form
any idea of the vast proportions of these ancient and
mysterious giants of the desert. Gazing upward,
glancing along from step to step, the eye becomes
weary with reaching the summit of these wonderful
creations. It is no easy task to realize either the
size or the age of these Pyramids; the Great Pyramid
is supposed to have been built 4,200 years before the
birth of Christ, and measures 732 feet on a side, with
a perpendicular height of 480 feet.

Many have been the ideas propounded as to the
purpose the pyramids were intended to serve, but it
is now a generally accepted fact that they were simply colossal tombs. .

21. Temple Sphynx and Great Pyramid.—At
a short distance from the foot of the Pyramid of
Cheops, in a deep, sandy hollow, stands the world-
famed Sphynx,—most mysterious of all mysterious
images, the watcher of the desert, "the father of
terrors." Its huge mass was covered with desert
sand again and again, in ancient times as well as in
our own days; only the head, decorated with the
royal coif, being left, gazing fixedly eastward.

The mutilated state of the face renders it impossible to trace the outline of the features with any
accuracy, but the general expression may still be

gathered, and is one of great placidity. Some
ancient writers speak of the face as "very beautiful,"
and of the mouth as "graceful and lovely, and as it
were, smiling graciously;" and one traveler mentions
the "exquisite proportions of the Sphynx's head"
as the most wonderful thing he had seen in all his
journeyings.

Old Arab writers regarded the Sphynx as a talis-
man to keep the sand away from the cultivated
ground, and tradition says that it was mutilated in
the fourteenth century, and that since this desecration
the sand has made great encroachments.

Thousands have gazed upon this face, while yet
perfect, in adoration, and other thousands in more
recent ages with mingled admiration, curiosity and
awe.

22. The Sphynx Excavated.—During recent years
the Sphynx has been compelled to reveal itself, and
stand confessed to daylight and curiosity. It has
been ascertained that it was hewn out of the solid
rock, and where the stone has not lent itself to the
form of the lion-body it has been supplemented with
masonry. The figure measures sixty-four feet from
the crown of the head to the pavement on which the
paws rest; the head itself measuring thirty feet from
the top of the forehead to the bottom of the chin,
and about fourteen feet across. The body is 140 feet
long.

An altar, three tablets, a lion, and numerous fragments were discovered in the space between the
paws; no entrance could be found, and it is probable
that the interior is of solid rock. The altar stood
between the two paws, and a stately flight of steps

led up to it. Through many successive centuries worshippers innumerable mounted these steps to pay homage to the Sphynx.

The Sphynx was the image of a mighty god—Hamarchis—the young light which conquers the darkness; the soul triumphing over death; fertility expelling dearth. Each Pharaoh regarded himself as the mortal incarnation of the sun-god; and therefore the kings selected the form of a Sphynx as expressing the divine essence in their nature. The attribute of irresistible physical strength was represented by the powerful lion-body; the highest intellectual power by the human head.

23. Pyramid of Sakkarah.—Turning our steps southward in a short time we reach the pyramid of Sakkarah, which is curiously built in stages or degrees. The degrees are five in number, diminishing in height and breadth toward the top. The height of the lowest story is thirty-seven feet, the entire height of the pyramid being about 190 feet. It is entirely stripped of its outer covering, so that the blocks of stone of which it is built stand out naked and irregular. This pyramid differs from the others in many respects; it is not set to the four points of the compass as they are; its base is not a square, and its interior construction is very peculiar. Immediately under the centre is an excavation in the rock, seventy-seven feet in depth and twenty-four feet square. The top of this is dome-shaped and was originally lined with wooden rafters; the bottom is paved with blocks of granite, and beneath is a rude chamber, the opening to which was concealed by a granite block, four tons in weight.

There is a wonderful fascination about this pyramid. One is never weary of looking at it, and of repeating to one's self that this is indeed the oldest building on the face of the whole earth. All we know of the builder is his name ; all we have of him is his pyramid, and these belong to the infancy of the human race.

24. Siout From the Nile.—We secure our dahabeeyah and begin our trip up the Nile, our first stop to be made at Siout, the capital of the province of the same name, and the residence of the governor of Upper Egypt. The Nile makes several large bends before reaching Siout, which often cause considerable delay. Indeed, after Siout is clearly in sight, and only three miles distant as the crow flies, following the long reaches of the river we often appear to be leaving it behind, the town itself, with clustered cupolas and arrowy minarets, lying back in the plain at the foot of a great mountain pierced with tombs.

Siout is famous throughout the country for its red and black pottery, which is of beautiful shape and excellent quality. There is a whole street of such pottery in the town, and our dahabeeyah is scarcely made fast before a dealer comes on board and ranges his brittle wares along the deck, while others display their goods upon the bank.

A lofty embanked road, planted with fine trees, leads to Siout, and many of the buildings are very attractive, but once in the heart of the town we find the thoroughfares dusty, narrow, unpaved and crowded. The houses are of plastered mud or sun-dried bricks, and altogether Siout, which from the distance looks like a vision of dreamland, on nearer acquaintance we find both ugly and ordinary.

25. Colonnade, Temple . of Denderah.—Continuing our journey up the Nile, we land to see the celebrated ruins of the temple of Denderah. From the distance the temple looks enormous—an immense low, sharply-defined ‑mass of dead-white masonry. The walls slope in slightly towards the top, and the facade seems as though supported on eight square piers, with a large doorway in the centre. All looks strangely solemn, more like a tomb than a temple.

A ride of two miles, over a plain covered with coarse, tall grass and with occasional clumps of palms, brings us to the temple. We find the facade to be composed of huge, round columns with human-headed capitals; and the massive gateway is rich with inscriptions and bas-reliefs. Not until we stand immediately under the ponderous columns do we realize the immense proportions of the building. The cornices and mouldings contain the richest curves; the capitals of the columns consist of a woman's face four times ‑repeated, which appears to smile on you from which ever side you regard it ; the sculptures represent scenes of joy and pleasure ; religious festivals, processions and groups, charmed by the sound of music ; fit subjects for a temple dedicated to Hathor, the Egyptian Venus, goddess of beauty and love.

26. Trading Boat on the Nile.—Our picture shows one of the common Arab boats of the Nile, such as are used for trading purposes. It is flat-bottomed and quite shallow in the hold ; the light draught being adapted to the numerous shoals in the river, and the necessity for towing on the banks when the wind is ahead. The lanteen sails have very long yards, and when a fleet of boats are going together before the wind the sails have a most singular and beautiful effect, for they seem like a flock of huge birds, with wings uplifted, as if about to take flight.

The Arab sailors have hard work and wretched fare. They all sleep on deck exposed to the weather, wrapped up in a course brown woolen robe, which is their bed by night, and their outer garment by day; it reaches the ankles and has wide, loose sleeves, and resembles a woman's dress rather than a man's. As they walk about or sit squatting upon the ground, the greater part of the lower order of Arabs look like old women in dirty and ragged brown cloaks. It seems odd enough to see sailors at work in this trim, yet they work hard at the rope when "tracking" the boat on shore, or on board when rowing or pushing with the pole. Their legs and feet are bare; they are all excellent swimmers and take to the water as readily as dogs, stripping themselves in an instant and plunging into the river to shove the boat, or to carry a rope on shore.

27. The Grand Temple of Luxor.—Our next stopping place is at Luxor, which occupies part of the site of the city of Thebes, the capital of ancient Egypt. Thebes was built on both sides of the river; a more noble site for a great inland city the world can hardly offer, and that site was occupied by a city, the wealthiest, most populous, and most richly embellished of any in the world. From each of its hundred gates two hundred war chariots could at once be sent out to repel the enemy. Its public buildings, its quays, its thousands of private edifices are gone, and have left few traces ; of its sacred edifices five large ruins are all that remain in evidence of its ancient splendor.

Luxor is a modern Arab village occupying the site of one of the oldest of these five ruins. The original sanctuary and the adjoining chambers, with the large colonnade and the pylon before it, were built by Amunoph III; Rameses II afterwards added the great court, the pyramidal towers, and the obelisks and statues.

Until quite recently it was impossible to trace the plan of this wonderful structure. The temple formed the nucleus of the modern village, and mud hovels, pigeon towers, dirty yards, and the village mosque clustered in and about the ruins. Stately capitols peeped out from the midst of sheds, in which buffaloes, camels, donkeys, dogs, and human beings were crowded together. The ordinary routine of Arab life. was going on amid winding passages that masked the colonnades, and defaced the inscriptions of the Pharaohs. Of late the ruins of the great temple have undergone a complete transformation. The mud hovels have been removed, and the temple stands revealed in all its grandeur of design and beauty of proportion. The great courtyard built by Rameses the Great measures 170 feet by 190, and our picture enables us to form some idea of the size of the massive columns which are fifty-seven feet in height.

28. General View of Luxor.—The village mosque is now the only one of the modern structures left within the temple. The great court, the pyramidal towers, and the obelisks, though last in the order of antiquity, form the commencement of the temple. The obelisks are of red granite, highly polished, the four sides covered with hieroglyphics, admirable alike for the style of their execution and the depth to which they are cut. But one of these obelisks remains in its place, its companion having been transported to Paris, where from its post of honor in the Place de la Concorde, it looks down on the gay life of the French capital.

Beside the obelisks were two sitting statues of Rameses, one on each side of the pylon or gateway. The whole outer surface of the towers is covered with elaborate sculptures of gods and men, horses and chariots, the carnage of war and the pageantry of triumph.

29. A Mummy Dealer.—Luxor is the great emporium for the sale of antiquities. Immediately upon your boat being moored under the bank, there is a general rush of donkeys and donkey-boys, guides, beggars, and antiquity dealers ; the children cry for backshish ; the dealers exhibit strings of imitation scarabs ; while the donkey-boys loudly call the names and praises of their animals. The dealers in "anteekahs" waylay and follow you wherever you go ; every man, woman, and child about the place is bent on selling you a bargain; and the bargain, in ninety-nine cases out of a hundred, is an imitation executed with such skill as to almost defy detection. A good thing is to be had occasionally, but a good thing is never shown as long as there is market for a poor one, and the dealer can readily discover whether the purchaser is experienced or otherwise.

The desire of every traveler's heart is to become the possessor of a mummy. The sale of mummies is prohibited by the government, and each one that is found is carefully forwarded to the museum at Boulak, —but of course, this fact renders the hunt all the more exciting, and to possess a stolen mummy becomes the acme of happiness.

After many precautionary arrangements, the purchaser is finally led to where the mummy is hidden in a rock-cut tomb; the sale being conducted with the greatest secrecy. There is a growing passion for mummies among Nile travelers; the price rises with the demand, and a mummy nowadays is not only a prohibited but a costly luxury. One traveler tells of some friends who secured a mummy "at an enormous price; and then, unable to endure the perfume of their ancient Egyptian, drowned the dear departed at the end of a week."

30. Avenue of Sphynxes and Propylon, Karnak.

Leaving the village of Luxor, we ride out across a wide plain, barren and hillocky in some parts, in others overgrown with coarse halfeh grass, indicating the site of ancient ruins; the road, uneven but direct, leading straight to Karnak. All at once the road widens and becomes a stately avenue, guarded by a double line of sphynxes, and led towards a lofty pylon, standing up clearly against the sky. Close beside this grand gateway is a thicket of sycamore palms, while beyond we see the twin pylons of a temple. The sphynxes are collossal, measuring ten fect in length. All are headless, some split asunder, some overturned, others so mutilated that they resemble torrent-worn boulders, yet enough remains to show that they were sculptured with exquisite art. The avenue once reached from Karnak to Luxor, and taking into account the distance from temple to temple, there cannot originally have been less than five hundred of these sphynxes. The effect upon one passing through the avenue must have been in the highest degree impressive and well calculated to compose the mind and prepare it for the worship of the gods to whom the temple was dedicated.

31. The Great Hall of Columns, Karnak.— Leaving the Temple of Rameses II., we turn toward the river and approach the Great Temple by way of its main entrance. We pass through what has once been another great avenue of sphynxes leading up from the grand landing place on the Nile. Passing through a tremendous portal we reach a large open court with a covered corridor on either side, and a double line of columns down the centre. Through another great propylon and we reach the Grand Hall, the largest and most magnificent of all the Egyptian monuments; a forest of gigantic pillars; this far exceeds in grandeur any other portion of the temple, and there is not in the whole world a hall which can be put in remotest comparison with it; the scale is vast, the effect tremendous. Six men, standing with extended arms, could barely span these columns round. They cast a shadow 12 feet in breadth,—such a shadow as might be cast by a tower. The rows of columns to right and left supported windows of stone trellis-work, reaching as high as the twelve large pillars, and the roof glittered with stars strewed on a blue ground.

32. General View of the Great Temple, Karnak. —At the end of the Great Hall is another propylon, much ruined, and beyond is a narrow, open court, where are two obelisks, which although they are 75 feet high, appear small in their position. One is thrown down and broken, but the other still stands. Passing through another propylon and another court we come to the great obelisk of Queen Hatasoo, the largest in the world.

Beyond this all is confusion; vast lengths of sculptured walls covered with wondrous battle subjects; ruined court-yards surrounded by files of headless statues; fallen columns, roofless chambers, shattered pylons are passed by and succeeded by fresh wonders. But in the midst of our admiration a shadow creeps o'er us and a sigh is borne on the atmosphere, as we remember at what a terrible sacrifice these buildings were erected, for every stone of these huge temples cost at least one human life.

33. The Colossi, Thebes.—Who has not heard the poetic tale of the Singing Memnon? How, as his mother, the rosy dawn appeared, and shed her tears —the morning dew—on the statue of her son, he gratefully greeted her with a soft song? This is the beautiful legend that the Greeks have woven around the northern of the two colassal figures which stand in the wide solitary plain, with the Libyan mountains as a background. The figures are between 50 and 60 feet in height, and about 40 feet apart: they are all that remain of the gigantic edifice erected by Amenophis in honor of his mother, his wife, and himself. The vast halls of the temple are totally destroyed, but the remains compose so huge a mass that we are justified in supposing that the Memnonium must have exceeded all the others in size and extent.

The sound emitted by the Memnon resembled the breaking of a harp-string or the ring of metal, and various opinions have existed as to whether the sound was the result of natural phenomenon or priestly craft. Both statues were originally one entire block, but the northern one was injured by an earthquake. The vocal phenomenon appears to have resulted from the action of the rays of the sun, which at first rising are very powerful in these latitudes; these, striking on the broad inclined surface of the statue while it was still wet with the dews of night, caused the particles of the stone to expand with a peculiar ringing noise. The portion of the colossus that had been thrown down was restored by Septimius Severus; the sounds ceased, and the "Harp of Memnon" was heard no more.

34. Great Court, Medinet Aboo.—A short distance from these collossal statues, and upon the ledge of rock which borders the plain and forms the base of the Libyan hills, is situated the Temple of Medinet Aboo. Next in importance to Karnak, and second in interest to none of the Theban ruins, this vast group of buildings is distinguished by the grandeur and originality of its plan, and the excellent preservation of its most important parts. The temple was constructed at different periods—the original edifice by one of the Pharaohs, but the more modern parts by the Ptolemies and Cæsars. More recently still one area has been converted into a Christian church, by erecting an altar and covering the pagan sculptures with plaster. The ruins consist of a small temple ; an exceedingly curious and interesting building, part palace, part fortress, generally known as the Pavilion; and a large and magnificent temple built by Rameses III. to commemorate his deeds of valor. The walls are covered with sculptures representing great wars, great victories, magnificent praises of the prowess of the king, pompous lists of enemies slain and captured, and inventories of precious gifts offered by the victor to the gods of Egypt.

35. The Rameseum Grand Hall, Thebes.—One of the noblest creations of Egyptian architecture was the Rameseum, the remains of which are a conspicuous ornament of Western Thebes. The walls tell the story of how, in a furious battle, Rameses the Great was cut off from his army, and how by the might of his own right arm he defended himself against the enemy, and setting himself again at the head of his forces, disastrously defeated the opposing army. To keep his own glorious deeds in remembrance, and as a thank offering to the gods, he erected this magnificent temple. Entering the first court, we find the statue of the king, once the largest statue in Egypt, now lying in fragments on the earth. It was hewn out of one solid piece of granite, and was 75 feet in height and 23 feet across the shoulders. One ear, which is still intact, is 3 feet

3 inches long, and the foot measures 11 feet in length by 4 feet 10 inches in breadth. This statue is one of the wonders of Egyptian workmanship, and although it repeats every detail of the colossi of Abou Simbel, it surpassed them in finish of carving and perfection of material. The stone is beautiful in color and close and hard in grain; the solid contents of the whole are calculated to have been 887 tons. How this immense mass was transported, how it was raised, and how it was overthrown are still questions for conjecture.

36. **Valley of the Tombs of the Kings.**—Before leaving Luxor we must visit the valley of the tombs of the kings. Going down the river bank some little distance, we cross a cultivated plain, and reach the foot of the rocky hills that border it. Before us opens a narrow pass, through which, in bygone ages, the mourning train followed the bier of the Pharaoh into the valley of death. It is closed in on both sides by bare walls of yellowish limestone; the weird rocks stand out like sentinels to right and left; the chalky track glares under foot; not a breath stirs; the intense heat of the sun pours down into the narrow and dismal gorge, and its rays falling on the rocks, heat them like the walls of a gigantic oven; all is desolation; not the smallest herb or blade of grass can strike root in these rocky cliffs. The gorge opens into a small plain, from which a ravine runs up into the mountain, and it is there we find the most ancient sepulchres of the kings. A few feet above the soil of the valley we see the opening of a tomb; then another; and yet more. The tombs are built on

the same general plan, but differ in the number and size of the rock-hewn chambers, and the number and finish of the inscriptions on the walls. All the inscriptions refer to the life to come ; the wanderings of the soul after its separation from the body, the the terrors and dangers that beset it during its journey through Hades, and the demons it must fight, are subjects of endless illustration.

37. Pylon of the Temple at Edfoo.—On the western bank of the Nile, surrounded by villages and hamlets, is the temple of Edfoo. From a distance we catch sight of the tall pylons, rising creamy in light, against a soft blue sky. A few years since nothing was visible of this great temple save the top of these pylons. The rest of the building was as much lost to sight as if the earth had opened and swallowed it. Its courtyards were choked with foul debris; its sculptured chambers were buried under forty feet of soil; its terraced roof was a maze of closely-packed huts, swarming with human beings, poultry, dogs, and kine. To-day the huge building stands before us in the sunshine, erect and perfect. The pylons, covered with gigantic sculptures, tower to a height of 115 feet. Through the great doorway, 50 feet in height, we catch glimpses of a grand court-yard, and of a vista of doorways, one behind the other. In these vast courts and storied halls all is unchanged ; every pavement, every column, every stair is in its place. The hieroglyphic inscriptions are as sharp and legible as the day they were cut. If here and there a capital has been mutilated, the blemishes are scarcely observed, and in nowise mar the wonderful effect of the whole

38. The Harbor of Assouan.—We journey southward for a distance of 68 miles to reach Assouan, the city of the cataract, and the frontier town of Egypt. The Nile here looks as if it had come to a sudden end, and the dahabeeyah is lying in a land-locked lake of beautiful outline. Opposite, the rocks and cliffs rise from the water, piled one upon the other. These, like all the rocks in this neighborhood, are of a shining reddish-brown, for we are here in the harbor of the ancient town of Syrene, the native land of syenite, and in the very heart of the great dyke of granite which protrudes westward as if on purpose to check the course of the Nile. The brave river has succeeded in breaking through its prison of rock at the first cataract, of which we hear the roar in the distance. Assouan is surrounded by palm groves, which completely conceal the lower part of the town, but not the grey houses of the higher quarter. From the eastern shore of the Nile where the town stands, rises a bold fragment of Moorish architecture with arches open to the sky. In the centre of the stream is the island of Elephatine, brightly and refreshingly green with its fields, shrubs, and palm trees.

39. First Cataract of the Nile.—We bid farewell to Egypt and enter Nubia through the gates of the first cataract, which is in truth no cataract, but simply a succession of rapids. The Nile here spreads itself over a rocky basin bounded by sandslopes on the one side, and by granite cliffs on the other. The course of the river is broken by a vast accumulation of granite boulders of reddish-brown color, whose polished surface shine like dark mirrors. Though our picture presents a very quiet appearance, the water rushes in divided currents, eddying and roaring through the rocky chasms.

At the time of the inundation, when all but the highest rocks are under water, the navigation is as easy here as elsewhere, but when the waters subside the paths are everywhere difficult and dangerous; and to this danger and difficulty the Sheykh of the Cataract and his crew owe their occupation. By the united efforts of many men, the use of much rope, and a system of double hauling the dahabeeyah ascends the rapids by sheer muscular force. Meanwhile the men rock their bodies with a peculiar swaying movement, chanting a wild accompaniment, and making as great a show of energy as though they were hauling the boat up Niagara.

40. Philæ from the Cataract.—Many of the islands of the cataract lying between Assouan and Philæ are most picturesque in structure and appearance. From one of these we obtain a fine view of Philæ, that loveliest of islands. The splendid buildings which stand on its soil; the delicious verdure that decks its shore; the laughing, sparkling waters of the river that has rescued it from the desert; the crown of granite peaks and boulders which form its rampart on the north; the smiling plain which turns its face to the south; and the glorious blue sky of this rainless region, never dimmed by a cloud—all, all unite to make this island a veritable place of enchantment. It was a true instinct that led the priests of Pharaonic times to dedicate this pearl of the Nile to the feminine divinity, Isis.

Philæ is now totally uninhabited, but there was a time when it was crowded with pilgrims and voyagers. The Pharoahs who were going forth to war against the people of the south came here to sacrifice and pray to the revered goddess; and it was the goal of numberless pilgrims from Egypt, by whom it was given its name signifying "the end."

It was the burial place of Osiris, called the "Holy Island;" its very soil was sacred ; none might land upon its shores or even approach too near, without permission. To obtain that permission and perform the pilgrimage to the tomb of the god, was to the Egyptian what the Mecca pilgrimage is to the pious Moslem of to-day.

41.   The Ruins of Philæ.—The island was occupied by one principal temple dedicated to Isis, and several subordinate chapels which clustered round it.   Nowhere has the mania of the Egyptians for irregularity been carried to such an extent as here.   No Gothic architect in his wildest moments ever played so freely with lines and dimensions, and none, it must be added ever produced anything so beautifully picturesque as this.   It contains all the play of light and shade, all the variety of Gothic art, with the grandeur of the Egyptian style.   The island is small, and the scale of the buildings has been determined by the size of the island.   Grace and proportion take the place of massiveness ; and the keynote of the whole is not magnitude, but beauty.   The twin towers of the propylon, covered with sculptures nearly as perfect as in the days of the Ptolemies who built them, stand out in unbroken lines against the beautiful azure sky.

As we pass through the propylon, and enter colonnades, and quadrangles, and chapels in succession,
our admiration increases, for nowhere else have we
seen such beauty and lightness, and such exquisite
coloring. The bas-reliefs on the walls, the intricate
paintings on the ceilings, the colors upon the capitals,
are all incredibly fresh and perfect.

Among the smaller buildings, and by far the most
famous, is that known as " Pharaoh's Bed," a pavilion
on the eastern bank of the island, standing out in the
pure and balmy atmosphere, a slender and airy
structure; a most perfect union of Greek and Egyptian
art.

42. Ruins of the Mosque Mishchod.—Sailing
gently southward from Philæ the broad current comes
on in one smooth, glassy sheet, unbroken by a single
rapid. The river curves away grandly to the right,
and vanishes behind a range of granite hills ; a simi-
lar chain hems in the opposite bank. A few mud
houses mark the site of a village, the greater part of
which lies hidden among the palms. High above
the palm groves fringing the edge of the shore is the
Mosque Mishchod, standing on its rocky prominence
like a castle on the Rhine. A desolate ruin, its
clumsy proportions are in striking contrast to the
delicate beauty of Philæ, still visible in the distance.
Beyond the village opens a vast valley of shining
sand, while the mountains come down to the very
water's edge, leaving only a small strip of alluvial
soil.

43. Shadoof and Sakkieh.—The character of the
country south of Philæ differs very materially from

that of Egypt. The hills coming very near the river frequently leave only a narrow strip of soil at the immediate bank on which the people depend for their scanty supply of food; and we realize more and more how entirely the lands which we call Egypt and Nubia are nothing but the banks of this one solitary river. When the Nile is low the land must be irrigated, and this is done by the use of the shadoof or the sakkieh.

The shadoof is worked on the lever principle. A little hollow is dug in the bank on a level with the river. Into this descends a bowl-shaped bucket, made of skin attached to a pole secured into an upright forked post. To the inland end of the post is appended a large lump of clay. The man who is working the shadoof takes hold of the cord by which the bucket is suspended, and bending down, by the mere weight of his shoulders dips it into the water. His efforts to rise gives the bucket full of water an upward impulse, which with the aid of the clay at the other end of the pole, lifts it to a reservoir into which it empties its contents. If the bank is steep other buckets and other reservoirs are needed, until the water is elevated to the top of the bank.

The sakkieh is a primitive machine consisting of two wheels, one set vertically to the river and slung with a chain of pots; the other a horizontal cog, usually turned by a buffalo. The pots go down empty, dip under the water, come up full and empty their contents into a reservoir or into irrigating channels. The sakkiehs are kept perpetually going and creak atrociously; their endless and melancholy noise is a delight to the native ; they creak, they howl, they groan, they squeal from morn till night and from night till morn ; hour after hour their melancholy chorus serves to make the night hideous, and to soothe the slumbers of the unfortunate traveler.

44. Gertasse.—Still traveling southward, we are impressed with the startling absence of life ; mile after mile drags its slow length along without any sign of human habitation. The desert is ever present ; the barren mountains press upon our path ; but it is no wonder that life should be scarce in a district where the scant soil yields barely food enough for those who till it.

About twenty-five miles south of Philæ we reach the village of Gertasse, a short distance north of which are the remains of what was once a magnificent temple dedicated to the worship of Isis. Now, alas ! but a few columns remain to tell us of its departed glory. How beautiful it must have been with the silver Nile flowing at its foot, the luminous blue sky overhead, and the golden sand of the desert as a background we can only surmise. Of the six columns still standing amid a mass of fragments, four show the characteristic lotus capitals, while the other two are adorned with the head of the goddess to whom the temple was dedicated.

45. Nubian Boy Riding Buffalo.—Though there exists no boundary line to mark where Egypt ends and Nubia begins, the nationality of the races dwelling on either side of that invisible barrier is as sharply

defined as though an ocean divided them. At the
cataract one comes suddenly into the midst of a
people that apparently have nothing in common with
the population of Egypt. They belong to a lower
ethnological type, and they speak a language derived
from purely African sources. To this day they are as
distinct and inferior a people as when the Egyptian
conquerors were wont to speak of them as "the vile
race of Kush." As we cross the border, too, we find
the buffalo superseding the camel for domestic purposes. Our young friend in the picture is dressed in
the usual costume of the children of Nubia, being
simply *in puris naturalibus;* for until they are about
twelve years of age their only article of apparel
consists of a cap. As they run along the banks of
the river, importuning you to buy an "anteekah" or
screaming for backshish, they look like little live
bronzes shining in the sun.

The men of Nubia usually wear only the loin
cloth ; and the complete costume of a Nubian lady
consists merely of a girdle of long fringe, made
of narrow strips of leather soaked in castor oil,
the top ornamented with shells and old brass but-
tons.

To the Nubian the odor of castor oil is delicious,
and he reckons it among his greatest luxuries. His
wives saturate their wonderfully plaited tresses in it;
his daughters perfume their fringes with it, his boys
anoint their bodies with it, and he himself, though
not otherwise very attentive to his toilet, does not
fail to rejoice in his shining shoulders. Happy the
traveler who can train his degenerate nose to delight
in the aroma of castor oil.

46. Kirscheh.—Still onward we move over the gleaming waters of the Nile until we reach the rock-hewn temple of Kirscheh. In many places in Nubia, where the mountains approach so near the edge of the river, the temples are excavated in the solid rock; sometimes, as in this case, a portico being built to the front. As we stand here in the great entrance to the temple, the collossal figures forming the facade cannot be seen, but from the frieze of the portico we can gather some idea of how rich in inscriptions this temple must have been. As we look before us words can scarcely do justice to the beauty of the scene. The curious mud houses on the bank of the river; the foamy sea-green of the palm tufts; the golden sand of the desert; the river, shining and beautiful; the pink haze of the distant mountains; unite to form a prospect that is like a scene from fairyland.

47. Temple and Desert, Wady Saboah.—Still pushing our way southward we reach Wady Saboah, where there is a solitary temple drowned in sand. This temple was erected by Rameses the Great, and was approached by an avenue of sphynxes and colossi, now shattered and buried, but originally made in the image of the builder. The roof is gone, the inner halls and the sanctuary are choked and impassable. Only the propylon stands clear of sand; and that, massive as it is, looks as if one touch of a battering ram would bring it to the ground. Every huge stone is loose, every block in the cornice seems tottering in its place.

The chambers afford some curious evidences of having been used as a Christian church. Over the god whose image was carved in the adytum has been plastered a picture of St. Peter; the other paintings however, have not been altered, and the result is that Rameses II. is now seen making offerings to a Christian saint.

48. Great Temple, Aboo Simbel.—Of all the wonders of Nubia, the Great Temple of Aboo Simbel is certainly the most marvelous. The artists took a mountain and hollowed and carved it as though it were a cherry-stone, and left it for feebler men of after ages to marvel at forever. One great hall and fifteen spacious chambers they hewed out of the heart of the rock; then smoothed the rugged precipice towards the river, and cut four huge statues with their faces to the sunrise, two to the right and two to the left of the doorway, there to keep watch to the end of time. These tremendous statues are 66 feet high, without the platform under their feet. They measure across the chest 25 feet 4 inches; from the shoulder to the elbow 15 feet 6 inches, and so on in relative proportion; if they stood up they would tower to a height of at least 83 feet.

The face is the most perfect handed down to us by Egyptian art. The last Rameses to the southward is the best preserved. The left arm and hand are injured, but with a few exceptions the figure is as whole, as fresh in surface, as sharp in detail, as on the day it was completed. The second is shattered to the waist; his head lies at his feet half buried in sand. The third is nearly as perfect as the first; while the fourth has lost not only the whole beard, but has both arms broken away, and a big cavernous hole in the front of the body

High in a niche over the doorway, standing 20 feet
in height, is a statue of Ra to whom the temple was
dedicated.

49. Interior of Great Temple.—Entering the
Great Hall we find eight colossi, four to the right and
four to the left, ranged down the centre, bearing the
mountain on their heads. Their height is 25 feet
With hands crossed on their breasts, they clasp the
flail and crook, emblems of majesty and dominion.
It is the attitude of Osiris, but it is the face of
Rameses the Great.

Beyond this first hall lies a second hall supported
on four square pillars; beyond this again, a transverse
chamber; last of all the sanctuary. The total depth
of the excavation is about 200 feet, and the effect of
the whole is vast, weird and mysterious.

The objects of greatest interest are the subjects on
the walls relating to the conquests of Rameses the
Great; the most stupendous historical record ever
transmitted from the past to the present. Scenes of
of war, of triumph, and of worship are before us.
All is the movement and splendor of battle. The
greatest wonder is the huge subject on the north
wall of the Great Hall; a monster battle-piece, covering an area of 25 feet by 57 feet, and containing over
eleven hundred figures.

50. Second Cataract of the Nile.—Still onward
we push our way along the life-giving river until we
reach the Second or Great Cataract, which extends
over a distance of many miles. It is impassable
except at one season of the year during the high

Nile. Like the first cataract it consists of a succession of rapids, with numerous black, shining rocks dividing the river into endless channels. The water foams, and frets, and falls; everywhere full of life and full of voices.

Southward the Nile stretches away, running like a silver thread through the desert waste.

This is the end of our journey. Loath are we to say farewell to this wonderful country and more than ready to verify the truth of the Oriental proverb which says: "Whoever has tasted the water of the Nile will long for it forever."